Whistle

Martin Figura

[signature]

*Kji lym
Sophoh 2012*

*arrowhead
poetry*

First published 2010 by
Arrowhead Press
70 Clifton Road, Darlington
Co. Durham, DL1 5DX
Tel: (01325) 260741

Typeset in 10pt Laurentian by
Arrowhead Press

Email: editor@arrowheadpress.co.uk
Website: http://www.arrowheadpress.co.uk

ISBN 978-1-904852-26-1

Printed by MPG Biddles Ltd., King's Lynn, Norfolk.

In Memoriam

June Evelyn Figura 1933-1966

for Helen

Acknowledgements

I owe special thanks to Helen Ivory and George Szirtes whose help with this book went far beyond their respective duties of wife and MA tutor. The book would not be here without them.

I would also like to thank: Andrea Holland for her support and encouragement, Jacob Polley and Matthew Hollis for their close readings and helpful criticism, Jackie Kay, Patience Agbabi and Francesca Beard for their time and kind comments, the Piggotts, my sisters Sue and Lindsay, first wife Dawn and the many friends who have helped and supported me along the way, especially Tom Corbett and my *Joy of 6* companions: Andrea Porter, André Mangeot, Anne Berkeley and Peter Howard.

And of course Joanna Boulter and Roger Collett of Arrowhead Press.

Some of these poems have appeared in the following magazines:
Envoi
nthposition
Seam
Veto
Poetry News
Same (USA)
The Rialto
Ink, Sweat & Tears

The Morning Room won the 2006 Café Writers poetry competition.

Jacket Illustration:

June Figura circa 1949

Contents

A Good Son
Prologue

This is mercy, and I a good son
You are my father, so never alone

This isn't pity, cold as a gun
Not a word will be written

Not a word will be written
This isn't a chisel pressed to a stone

This isn't pity, cold as a gun
You are my father, so never alone

Let this be mercy, and I a good son

Love Letters
(June to Frank 1949-51)

*I bought a dream of a coat darling, a loose one in gabardine. ...I owe mum
the money out of her insurance, but I will pay it back and besides I had to
have a loose coat.*

June stands on the bedroom lino,
wraps her gaberdine coat around her.

She lets the wardrobe mirror
take her dreams and turn them silver.

*We didn't go to the pictures over the weekend, not that I missed the films, but
I could have rested my head on your shoulder and schmoozed a little.*

Passport to Pimlico flickers
onto the silver screen and June
is lost to her own country.
They are King and Queen
on thrones of velvet. Stars
swirl above their heads.
They turn to each other
and kiss and kiss.

*If I had the money, I would catch a train to Shrewsbury tonight. Frank
darling I love you so much it is impossible to wait for twelve months, I
cannot do it darling. I want you to ask Mum again and if she says no, break
it to her gently that we are going to apply to the magistrates.*

She reaches her white-gloved hands
across the refreshment room table.
They don't notice the rain outside,
nor the other couples parting
and meeting. He tells her again
with that dark accent, that he loves her
and it's like her heart has stopped,
like nothing could be forbidden.

*I want it to be nice, to go to bed without curlers. We can pretend we are
married.*

There is only enough moonlight
for the shape of him. She learns
by touch. Afterwards her head spills
black curls onto his chest. The sound
of their breathing fills the room.

I still want a peach, but I have no hope of getting one.

There in the middle of a white plate
in the middle of the table, a peach
in the glow of its own light. It's for her
and how he got it he will never tell;
only say that in China
it is the name given to a young bride
and a symbol of everlasting life.

*I shall keep the house nice and have the water ready for your wash and have
your clothes ready to change and your slippers by the fire. While you're
getting washed and changed I can have your tea on the table.*

A whole day slips through the pale purple
of Mansion Polish. A carpet sweeper
chases specs of dust through lavender fields.

Her own face appears in the furniture.
She shines small brass animals back to life.
A tiny kitchen disappears into the mist

of an afternoon. A sponge cake rises
behind the oven door. He watches
the last slow hour on the factory clock.

*...we can nurse baby for half an hour and then you must put him to bed. I
insist on this as I want him to know his Daddy as much as me. He must
grow up to love us equally. We must give him a good life so he will be proud
of us.*

11

Born

my mother calls me to the world
from the thud
of my hidden room

a gush of water
the muscular push

I am a boy
skin
slick as celluloid

my first focus
an iris
an aperture dilating
a click

everything is light

Mother

As its representative on earth she sets
the lemon meringue onto the cloth -
its perfect roundness and snowy peaks.

She divides it up with the cake knife,
cuts through the sweet crust
into the bright tartiness beneath.

We devour it; lick every last crumb
from around our mouths,
leave a shining empty plate.

How to Steal

I can be trusted on my own for a few minutes.
First off, a big spoon of Andrews in a glass
followed by orange squash and water - instant pop,
then the loaf and carving knife.

Cutting soft white bread isn't easy when you're seven,
you do your best - two ragged doorstops.
Rewrap the bread and put the knife back
exactly where you found it.

Drag the bread across the margarine a couple of times,
pick off the crumbs, thump ketchup
onto the middle of one slice, place the other
on top and move them around - you don't want washing up.

Leg it up the garden before mum returns from the shop,
gobble down the buttie behind the shed,
stroll back in through the kitchen door
as cool as you like.

Don't blink when she takes her hankie
and wipes the sauce from the corner of your mouth.

Big Sister

Tonight the click, click, click
of stilettos on the pavement
sounds like rattlesnakes
in your sock drawer, if your sister
tells you that's what she put in there.

I send for mother with a howl.
She lifts me to the window, shows me
the high-heeled ladies passing by.
When she's gone, I hear my sister
hissing behind the door.

Fire-Place

Father tapped in each careful stone
to the satisfaction of the spirit level.
We placed icons on its mantelpiece.

In return for warmth it demanded fuel
so each night father took to his knees
and made offerings of sticks and coal.

He became our Fire-God, took the vinyl
armchair as his throne, sat there
nursing the jawbone of an ass.

Glue

Dad covers the table with newspaper
while I rattle back from the shop,
the Airfix kit jumping in its box.

We spread out one hundred
and twenty two black plastic pieces,
match them to the tissue-paper plan.

The little man is stuck to his seat
and the whole thing built around him,
rough edges carefully sandpapered away.

He sits there now, his painted-on face
lost behind windows clouded grey
with our glue fingerprints.

Piano Practice

In the front room
the encyclopaedias
hide behind their facts;

the budgerigar
tucks his head
under his wing

and Polish crystal
tinkles hysterically
in its cabinet.

The piano has attempted
to conceal itself
behind the standard lamp

and wishes
for a thick coat of dust.

Numbers

I am a sharp yellow seven, prime and primary
I already know numbers are the law

My classmates drown in the five times table
While I race on in my head

   Five seventeens are eighty five
   Six seventeens are one hundred and two

Fountain Pen

If you are going to be a doctor,
you need to have a proper pen.

*

At WH Smith, in a ceremony
of the utmost gravity, my father
and the girl behind the counter

bestow the pen upon me.
Its rests on my palm,
marbled barrel fully loaded.

*

Black Quink Ink

when released from its bottle
will seep into your skin
through the pockets of your
new school shorts. Or else

mark you up for fingerprinting
before flying across the room
in a wodge of blotting paper.

*

Nibs suffer

when gouged
into desk lids.

Splayed and bent
they tear at exercise books,

scratching out
spelling mistakes.

*

We all know, that a pen should be kept
in a pencil case in your satchel. But

at times, for convenience, you will leave it
on a wall, or stuff it in your pocket, so later

it can slip out onto a bus seat, if it hasn't already
fallen into the grass during a handstand.

*

By the third purchase, all the pomp
has gone from the ritual.

My father carries out the transaction
in quiet disappointment.

Even the girl at Smith's
is exasperated with me.

On the bus home, it's explained
how carelessness, could, one day
cost a patient their life.

*

By the second week, the idea
that you have no homework
is becoming difficult to sustain.

Parents aren't stupid; teachers aren't stupid
and very soon they're going to get together on this.

Of course, if one, or both of your parents
were to die in a terrible accident, then
the small matter of homework would be forgotten.

No one would mind if you asked for a new pen.

Teach Yourself German

Every few weeks he would take the book
yellow and black, down from the shelf
and put its words in my mouth like a hook.

He started with numbers - acht, zehn, zwölf
hoping I'd recognise the taste,
find in it something of myself.

I explored the shape of them, traced
my ancestry with the tip of my tongue,
sucked their coating of sticky almond paste

back into my throat, where it clung
acht, acht, acht, neither swallowed
nor spoken, remained unsung.

Victor

'True Stories of Men at War'

As fathers stroll home from work
there is no birdsong and the November light
is all but gone.

Small boys run amok in avenues,
take cover behind privet hedges -
the smell of cordite, heavy in the air.

Over the traffic, the sound of battle:
grenades whistling overhead, the sporadic
rattle of toy guns from doorways.

At tea time, those whose turn it is
break cover, make a zigzagging run for it
shouting - ACHTUNG ACHTUNG.

They go down in a hail of bullets,
competing for the most dramatic death.
The pavement is so littered with Germans

that men must pick a way through
to reach their gates and take their sons
down paths into quiet houses.

Exile

Sometimes he comes home with Polish sausage
And a heart from another time and place
He serves it up with pickled cabbage

The journey here was no easy passage
A dismantled life thrown down a staircase
Sometimes he comes home with Polish sausage

There are certain kinds of knowledge
Time and distance can't erase
He serves it up with pickled cabbage

Exiles don't pack their own luggage
There's dead weight in every suitcase
Sometimes he comes home with Polish sausage

Snapshots have kept him hostage
His story frayed like a bootlace
He serves it up with pickled cabbage

He's had to learn another language
Wear it like a different face
Sometimes he comes home with Polish sausage
He serves it up with pickled cabbage

Silesia

A wife and three children, then
you can visit. It's twenty years
and there are still bomb holes
in the road. You bring back

Polish crystal for the cabinet,
brass inlaid wooden boxes
and tankards carved out of coal.

You take a thousand photographs;
one of a fallen horse being flogged,
not making a sound.

Journey 1965

Halfway between my father's birthplace
and mine I stand on the edge of a platform
as the night train swallows me up
in steam and noise. I can taste fire.

In Berlin, we're woken by floodlights.
Soldiers with machine guns come aboard,
open compartment doors and check papers.
I hold on tight to my Man from U.N.C.L.E.
membership card as we cross to the East.

*

The train stops in the middle of nowhere.
We climb down to our suitcase in the grass,
wave until the train disappears. The lane
is lined with cherry trees. From time to time
we rest on the bank, side by side like partisans
our eyes closed into crimson. We eat cherries
warm as blood and spit the stones over our heads.

At the farmhouse geese and piglets
chase me squealing through the trees.
Later, on hard benches, we eat and the talk
goes on above my head in Polish. I can hear
and smell the cattle through a slatted wooden door.
The dog's bowl, a German helmet, clatters
on the stone floor and is licked clean.

*

A man walks into the tenement courtyard
with a chicken under his arm. He has an axe
in his hand and is soon surrounded by children.
The chicken pecks a boy's head – *owa owa.*
The man does it quickly, his big hand holding down
the chicken's neck on the wood block, then
chop. The chicken runs for it, splashes our shins
with blood; its head on the cobbles stares at us.

*

I have put an empty shell upside down
into Opa's egg cup. It is a great joke
and Oma is beside herself as he shakes out
his napkin as usual. His spoon smashes
the empty egg and he throws his arms up
in mock horror. Oma's hands come together
in prayer; her eyes look up to St Anthony
on the wall, she is hopping from foot to foot.

*

Poosh pooosh Oma's bony hands
make space in the tram for us.
I spend the journey in the dark,
lost in black dresses and the smell
of cabbage. At the other end
old women spill out and race up
the church steps like beetles.

*

On the last day I am bought a watch
with seventeen jewels. My father
puts it in my blazer pocket, tells me
to keep it there till the end of the journey.
Only then can I set it going,
feel its heartbeat, check my pulse.

Coal

Caverns of fire growl deep underground
crack open the contaminated surface

so the murmur of voices can escape. The bones
of dukes and peasants, Bohemians, Prussians,

Mongol raiders and Moravians are pressed tight
into a fault line thin as a flag. The flag is the colour

of blood cells. Behind the buckling crosses
of window frames old men are dismantling clocks

on kitchen tables, looking for providence
amongst cogs and spiders.

And the black hills will join the sky and rain,
will pour down and bury this place.

Litany

Words pour like chemicals
into his burning throat, his head
becomes a swaying thurible,
incense smoke seething through
his teeth.

> *She is a Protestant*
> *She is unfaithful*
> *She is poisoning me*
> *Sie ist protestantisch.*
> *Sie ist treulos.*
> *Sie vergiftet mich*
> *She is a Protestant*
> *She is unfaithful*
> *She is poisoning me*

She feeds him eyes
until his stomach aches.
They grow claws and tongues,
climb his spinal cord, scrape
at the inside of his skull.

Glove

My mother and I pose in Sunday best
in front of a cottage with roses
around the door. She dreams

it is our house, where white gloves
will not be smudged or snagged on a thorn
and be left with a pin-prick of blood.

I could print this photograph
so dark, there would only be
her hand on my shoulder.

In my Parents' Bedroom

On this spring night the curtains burn
with distant fires.

The ceiling is blank sky,
the wallpaper a rose garden.

The dressing table's arms are full
of fallen objects, its mirror dumb.

Through the wall, it causes no more than a ripple
on the surface of milk.

My toy soldiers are stilled
and I dream on, not of a pale throat,

a kitchen knife, a pyjama cord
pulled tight.

The News

The whole thing tips upside down
at the news. Cups and saucers
spin away - disappear
into the infinite Artex swirl.

I am in the middle of the room,
the centre of a small universe
equidistant, not just from the walls
but the floor and ceiling too.

I begin a slow shadowless rotation
through the silence, heads are planets:

       the doctor's few thin hairs
       the rings of Saturn,
       Uncle Alan is the ginger sun,
       my sisters and I small lost moons,

       Auntie Margaret's cloud cover,
       Uncle Philip's oil fields,
       Father Lightbound's black jacket
       shouldering its own Milky Way.

Vanishing Point

The rear window flickers into life as we pull away,
the uncertain image of a boy on a bicycle appears,
behind him a painted backdrop of the avenue,
its sycamore trees and pebble-dashed houses:

Piggotts', Mitchells', Mrs Donnelly's with all
its confiscated footballs, her poodle yapping
at the fence. Children's games are caught
in mid-air, at the height of their action.

Uncle Philip turns onto the busy road. The boy
pedals like mad to stay with us, but we stretch away
and leave him stranded, disappearing.

Then there is just white light
and the loose flapping sound
of a film end escaping its gate.

The boy who

came down
the helter-skelter
bend after bend
has gone.

Keep this last film
dark and tightly rolled,
hold its tongue
between your teeth;
its boiled down bones
and animal hides,
its twenty layers of celluloid.

In the Car

Hippies making daisy chains
on the central reservation
ought to get a job.

Pakistanis pushing prams
on the pavement
look so happy here.

The Beatles
on the push button radio
need a haircut.

Uncle Philip and Auntie Margaret
in the front seats
of the Humber Super Snipe.

Uncle Philip at The Glass Factory

Sweating with the men in the jungle heat
of the factory floor, a glob of glass
fizzes through his coat and suit into the meat
of his arm. The shock rushes through his veins,
takes his shape and becomes cold to the touch.

A volcanic shift in his landscape has begun.
He takes to carrying a spoon to tip molten glass
down the nape of his neck and into the gaps
between shirt buttons. Soon this isn't enough
and he wades into its boiling fury.

Now only his hands and head have skin,
the rest of himself is hidden away
under clothes buttoned up to his chin.

Snowfall

Mass passed me by in a daydream
about running away to live in a cave,
rabbit skins keeping me warm.

Walking home from church, my shoes
with the secret compass in one heel
leave animal prints in the snow.

You really do see stars in the sudden
sickening darkness of a bang to the head.
It takes a while to work out what, if anything

is hurt. The taste of blood first,
then a fierce wave of pain from a tooth
through a lip. I am dangling like a puppet

Uncle Philip's hand on the collar
of my navy blue mac. Back in the house
it really begins to hurt.

Morning Room

The family sits round the table
ready for the meal, which is me
trussed up at the ankles and wrists,
cooked to a golden finish like a chicken.

Uncle Philip as head of the family
sharpens the knife, carves slices
of flesh from my thighs and deftly
transfers them to oven-warmed plates.

Now everyone gets stuck into the broccoli
and potatoes. They are pouring gravy,
spooning stuffing from my rib cage.

Breath

The harmonium wheezes
as June summons its reedy voice.

Her insistent foot works the pedal
and one sigh follows another

to explore the dim bedroom,
brush over the sleeping boy's face.

Her polka-dot veil shifts as she sings
O Breathe on me, O Breath of God

The boy wakes, inhales morning air
invisible and familiar as belief.

Evidence

Skin scraped from under June's white nails
into a polythene bag.

Skin under Frank's coarse chest hairs
broken by scratch marks.

Under his white shirt and black tie:
stratum corneum, stratum spinosum, stratum basale.

Trip to The Admissions Ward

The nurse puts a gentle hand into the small
of Frank's back, holds the other out, palm up
for him to take, whispers that she will lead.

The fluorescent lights blur as Frank is spun away
down the white corridor. The doors full of grinning faces
flash past, the clapping gets faster and faster.

The nurse's keys crash like a tambourine against her hip.
People shout his name, slap him on the back
as he passes. The ward is strung with bunting.

Frank sits dizzily on his bed to read all the cards,
while coloured balloons bob on ribbons
from the window bars. This is quite a welcome.

The Bath

Crow-eyed nurses watch the faint echo of a man
in six inches of bath water, silver-white lithium
drifts metallic through his blood stream, the span
of his hand in front of his face takes the low hum
from his mouth, returns it as a pebble to his tongue
for him to swallow, keep in the swim of his belly
below the muffled drum of his heart with all the rest.

The Weight

Frank moves as if he were full of stones
and the room a river, numb cold shoving
against his legs. The crow-eyed nurses
want to know how much of him is left.

He feels a thumb under his jaw, is lifted.
Scales accept the load, its muscle, its breath,
its knuckle bones.

Counting

Patients through a door, peas on a plate, knives, forks,
spoons, keys on a belt, pills in a plastic cup, minutes
in a day, sixty dormitory beds, heads on pillows, shouts
in the night, the distance from your neighbour, monsters
on the ceiling, therapeutic kicks, privileges, what is lost,
nurses' jokes, bricks in a wall, the number of steps
round the yard, jigsaw pieces, one small square of sky.

Day Room

Frank sits down, straight-backed
and stares ahead, not noticing
the TV's whine or the clatter
of the table tennis. He opens
his mouth and a beam of light
comes out, cuts through the smoke
and hits the blank wall opposite.

A boy with a bicycle, boys behind
school desks - one with a cross
marked above his head, a soldier
waving from a train, a bear in a zoo,
a ship, Buckingham Palace, a young man
in a pub with a girl, a wedding day,
a baby in a Silver Cross pram, a worker
in overalls, a children's birthday party,
a first holy communion, a holiday,
a day out at the castle,
a pebble-dashed house.

Language

His languages return
all at once as thoughts.

He tries to speak them.
Tongues slip from his mouth,

lash themselves tight
across his face.

The Machine Shop Broadmoor Hospital

Frank at work, hanging smoke, yellow light,
the noise of hammers, hot dust in his throat.

Engine Lathe Operations and Controls

The pleasure of precision, of calibration tools,
the cool shine of gauge wheels.

The spindle rotates in both directions.
The tail stock can be positioned along the ways

A cast gripped in a machine's jaws, a carbon tip
dead-centre, burrows to its glowing heart.

and the quill moves within the tail stock.
The carriage also moves along the ways.

Skeins of steel at his feet,
all their sharp edges.

The cross slide moves
perpendicular to the ways.

Small black cuts snag in his overall pocket,
fingerprints smudge a white china mug.

To keep some of the mechanisms moving
longitudinally straight and true,

His rough fingers turn a hand-made cigarette,
his tongue wets the gum-edge of a Rizla.

ways are machined on the top surface.
Ways are ground and often hardened.

He leans back in satisfaction, inhales,
talks with other men of countersinking.

New Boy

Curious, boys nudge against me.
Jaws lined with small white teeth
chew on bubble gum.

The inevitable puncture of sickly air
and I'm wrapped in their membrane
like a struggling pupa.

Over the weeks, I pick at it,
roll it under my thumb into grey lumps,
pull strands from my hair.

I drench my hands and arms
in saliva, run them over my face,
emerge in their image.

Chapel

This boy was smaller than all of us,
his skin pale and dry like his own breathing;
no wonder his father died.

We pray for him as solemnly as we can,
hang our young puzzled heads,
screw our eyes tight shut.

Afterwards I stay, pour out my own fat tears
onto the pew in front where they gather
to form a lake and then a waterfall spilling down

to the stone floor, where they gather again,
rise up the walls until the chapel becomes a bell,
each tiny sound amplified; the hiss of candles,
my gulps for air as the altar cloth passes over me.

My breath rides in bubbles to the surface and breaks.

Goalkeeper

Last to be picked and put in goal
toe-capped boots half way up
my sparrow shins like mop buckets.

Boys chase the ball towards me, each bounce
a body hitting the ground. My shoulder blades
crack apart, I breathe out small fast clouds
and crouch. Everything stops:

> the blood in my veins,
> the eyes in my head,
> the girl on the swing
> at the top of her arc,
> the dog and the stick,
> the man and the boy,
> the child in the pram,
> the yell in its throat,
> the cars in the street,
> the ball in the air,

the ball in my hands, coarse stitching
under my fingertips. The noise of the park.

Mary

Just boys and monks,
no girls in this universe.

That was until Mary from the village
found us in the out of bounds wood
and kissed us one by one. After that
we went down there all we could.

Mary did her stuff, until the night we heard
the unmistakable sound of monks
moving through the trees. Then came
spanking, letters to parents, sermons.

At night we lay awake
under our sheets.

Afternoon Tea with Father Hugh

He closes his eyes to think how he might
put it to me. I trace a line of cherryade
over the white cloth with a straw.

The icing on the bun is as pink as his round face,
a cigarette rests on his lip. *They've gone to Canada*
he says - *Uncle Philip and Auntie Margaret.*

I'll be going to the Vineyard at the end of term;
Mulberry Cottage. I picture it with roses around the door,
sweet dough sticking to the roof of my mouth.

He stubs out his cigarette
and lights another one.
I could have had whatever I wanted.

Thank You

Thank you Auntie Margaret
Uncle Philip - God bless
For avoiding any awkwardness
For leaving just like that

For sparing yourselves the upset
By getting school to tell us
Thank you Auntie Margaret
Uncle Philip - God bless

For not troubling us with regret
For not giving comfort your address
For bothering to care less

For going to Canada on a jet
Thank you Auntie Margaret
Uncle Philip - God bless

The Boy I Wanted to Be

If the top of his head
were hinged, I'd tip it open
reach in
delve about in the gloop
behind those blue eyes
un-knit the scar
from his glamorous cheek
steal the silver
from his tongue
pull out his easy manner
thread by thread
shove my arm
down his neck
relieve him
of his good heart
put my mouth
round his wind-pipe
suck out his breath.

Strange Boy

We believe there is a one in ten chance
the boy will inherit it from his father
The boy is top in maths
He is near the bottom of the class in everything else
He writes wild imaginative essays with little regard
for spelling or grammar
He cries easily
The boy's house number is Belmont 47 (a prime number)
We know he steals, but are letting it go for now
We also know he smokes
He pulls a face when he concentrates
The other boys have noticed this
The boy is left here during half-term breaks
He occupies himself with dice games of cricket and football
that can take days to complete
They are too complex for anyone else to participate in
The boy maintains a number of statistical graphs
He is a good goalkeeper
He has made some friends through football
He has invented an elaborate past
He carries a *1966-67 News of The World Football Year Book* at all times
Father William lets him complete his pools coupon
He has had some small successes

Touch

Stories pulled apart,
gristle stretched
and snapped, blood
drained away, a ghost.

My sisters and I
placed out of touch,
our own small diaspora.

The Camera

is inside a box, inside a box, inside
a padlocked room inside a warehouse.
I imagine it imagines itself forgotten,
left for dead in a town I'm pretty sure
it wouldn't recognise; that maybe
the town itself is forgotten,
boarded-up and wind-blown.

Its thoughts are brittle and unresolved.
One day I shall hold them with white gloves,
carefully brush away the dust and look
through their shadows and fingerprints.

Vineyard Boys

We are, we are the Vineyard Boys
We all wear the same shit shoes
We have broken all our toys
We are, we are the Vineyard Boys

We are cuckoos
We are noise
We are, we are the Vineyard Boys

We are issues, rent-boys, dole queues
We are, we are the Vineyard Boys

Mouth

A switch flicked
in the pit of a stomach
a pointless point
nitpicked
an argument running amok
can of petrol in hand
a match being struck

Liz

Centre-forward at the park
queen of the toe-poke
and shoulder-barge

Lady Madonna on Thursday nights
dances to Top of the Pops
in black and white

Pie Sucker

The sound of steak and kidney
sucked through a hole

All gummy grin
and gravy chin
he tags along
on skinny legs
of ringworm welts
and midgie bites

Gonk

Head-butter
Nutter
Culprit
Catholic
stole a stuffed bear
from Woolies
legged it

Someone *actually* shouted
STOP THIEF

He was cornered
by the Great British Public

Paul

Went to the shop
for tartan paint
stood for an hour
while you fetched
a long wait

One day
he left in a car
and didn't come back

Martin

Stuck up
too clever by half
doesn't fold his pyjamas
all boarding school
la-di-dah

Cakehole

Once a day, for the benefit
of a small crowd, he taps out
a No6 from a pack of ten,
sticks it in his gob, shapes

one huge hand against the wind,
runs his other chewed thumb
down the lighter wheel, flinging
a spark into petrol, into a flame,

an intake of breath, the sulphur
burn of white to grey, the hush
of the crowd, as in a single drag
he turns a whole cigarette to ash.

We are, we are the Vineyard Boys
We all wear the same shit shoes
We have broken all our toys
We are, we are the Vineyard Boys

We are cuckoos
We are noise
We are, we are the Vineyard Boys

We are issues, rent-boys, dole queues
We are, we are the Vineyard Boys

John Lennon's Rolls Royce

I wait for Maureen in the hall
of the Flora Dugdale Home for laughing girls,
girls who take it in turns to peer round the door
at the boy in the stifling yellow polo-neck.

We flee, blood-cheeked, turn the corner
before we hold hands, catch our breath, speak.
I take her to see John Lennon's
psychedelic Rolls Royce. It rains.

It rains so hard we are soaked
and she slips on the muddy verge.
In the bus shelter: Maureen's tartan skirt
stuck to her legs, me fiddling with its silver safety-pin,
the lurch for a kiss, the taste
of Trebor Mints, rain.

Messengers

I am cornered in the wilderness of streets
- they must have been watching over me.
One of them pushes me in the chest,
brings me down with a fist for the kicking.

They are angels alright, their duffle coats
are dusted with pollen and bulked out
by concealed wings. I can taste honey
and hear the sound of a badly played harp.

Call

In their house, ornaments
bought for a few pence
on the mantelpiece, like porcelain.

In their garden, an aviary
for all the wounded
flightless birds they've found.

I send out sound-waves
under the hum of power lines,
silent as the mouths of fish.

Piggotts

Taken prisoner by this bashing clouting clan. Jammed between
Danny and John, the second and third boys with their shock
white hair and flying fists. Dragged through lanes and hedges
into ponds and up trees for birds' eggs. Thrown into the gritty-
eyed dawn for mushrooms big as dinner plates and damsons
for damson jam. Put to work with sandpaper on rusting scrap-
heap cars. Flying over fields on the Honda Fifty, being chased
by the mad dog. The mad dog burying bones in your bed;
hurling itself downstairs, sticking its head up women's skirts.
Dianne as look-out while we skinny dip in the River Weaver
and once a water-rat swam between us. Dianne goes to
the Grammar; Billy crashed his Lambretta and then his Capri,
went to Spain with his mates.

      Holidays on Shell Island - *famous for its shells* - :
pitching into the air off dunes, racing the tide, screaming from
cliff tops, hauling crabs from the sea on twine on pop bottles,
diving into waves, digging a tunnel in the sand, me buried
alive, recovering in the tent's strange orange light listening to
Day of The Triffids on the radio.

      Friday night with Woodpecker Cider watching the
Hammer Horror film, falling asleep before the end. Week-ends
visiting family in terraced houses, everyone crowded into front
rooms: our Jeannie, our Gracie, Mooch, Auntie Annie and her
Ian. The grown ups smoking as if their lives depended on it.
The girls hitting as hard as the boys. Auntie Alice's and Uncle
Eddie's: their two lads playing Rolling Stones' records upstairs,
home-brew in every cupboard, under the sink, in the glory-hole,
in the out-house, in the greenhouse, in the wardrobe
- *come and have a taste of this lad* - brown ale, bitter, brandy,
marrow rum. Auntie Alice dolloping out steaming dinners
that make your belly pop.

      Being altar boys on Sunday mornings, then Checkley
for eggs and Cheshire Cheese from Len, his boots by the fire.
Him talking slow, Edie – his sister - busy at the stove. Home
in Henry the big black car, tinned tomatoes on toast
in front of the telly.

Family parties at the drop of a hat: party cans and egg-
rolls, trifles and crisps, hokey-cokeys and terrible dancing
to Status Quo, Auntie Lizzie's monologue. Us boys trying
for cool in market bought Ben Sherman's, brogues and two-
tone Sta-Prest, reeking of Brut; dancing with our cousins.
Aunt Jane a little merry lifting her skirt up her leg and shouting
look half a knicker. Three-card brag and poker for pennies.
Auntie Annie popping round next day on her moped for a chat.

    Pate, we call him that, loves watching *The Onedin Line*,
building dreamboats in the garden, boozing in The Derby Arms
(a room behind the shop). Sometimes he takes us with him
and tells stories about Australia, where Bill was born, where he drove
oil tankers across the outback and didn't see another soul for days,
not even a mirage, fixed the pedal with a block of wood
and fell asleep at the wheel. Once he tried to tell us the facts of life,
but couldn't. He reads *Exchange and Mart* and JT Edson books:
A Town Called Yellow Dog, The Law of the Gun, A Horse Called Mogollon.
He lies under old cars in the new clothes we've bought
to smarten him up. He does what Besse tells him most of the time.

    Besse rules us all with a tongue of iron, hands out advice,
dishes out justice, hands out love, fights for us all, watches the telly
with a silver cat on her lap, drinks ginger wine and smokes menthol
cigarettes, likes green and lets anyone in the house for a cup of tea.
One day I'll come home on leave and the taxi-driver will ask
what is that place?

Swimming

They teach me
to swim
in cold water.

I jump through
the meniscus,
my limbs

striking out
at the slow
blue molecules.

Little Angel

I will be a good boy here.
I promise I will never dawdle.
I'll do as I'm told, have no fear.

Be assured there's nothing queer
about me. I will be no trouble,
I will be a good boy here.

I believe in all that you hold dear
whatever it is, I will not quarrel,
I'll do as I'm told. Have no fear

of untidiness or dirt behind my ears.
It's no longer my nature to be idle.
I will be a good boy here

and now I'm in the second year
I will not lose my new satchel.
I'll do as I'm told, have no fear.

Even though my brothers jeer,
please call me your little angel.
I will be a good boy here,
I'll do as I'm told, have no fear.

Outside

After the car rounds the bend
Frank looks in the rear-view mirror
and there it is following behind

in a cloud of red brick dust. Later
he observes it from his window,
its gothic walls and water tower.

In time he'll get used to the shadow,
no longer need to draw his curtains
or drown its murmurings with the radio.

Record

Every second Saturday scruffy men
(and some women) place bric-a-brac
onto trestle tables in the church hall
with their fat hands.

My father keeps a poker-face,
gets what he wants for a thrilling
three pounds fifty.
He would have gone to a tenner.

At home, he puts the Dansette
on the floor, plugs it in
even before he removes his jacket.
A thumb over the left breast

of the fraulein on the album cover.
He slides out the black vinyl,
places the needle onto his reflection
and it hisses. He stands in the middle

of the room. Oompah music thumps
through the soles of his feet.

The open window,
the smell of a pine forest.

Home to Tea

The girl I'm going to marry
sits with a cup of tea on her lap
while Dad fusses over the gravy,
peels the potatoes under the tap.

She's good at small talk, admires
what he's done with the flat,
teases him about liking the flowers,
asks where he bought his jacket.

Later he fetches the camera
from the drawer in the wardrobe,
poses us on his sofa,
in case we never come back.

Fish

I throw a few crumbs, then feel your weight
as you snatch at my barbarous line.

You mouth and mouth as if trying to explain.
All I get is maggoty river-breath. The gilt

of your scales dull in the air. A thumbnail
could easily split your soft underbelly, spill your guts.

I give you back to the river,
its current of brown water.

Nerve Ends

I don't have my father's
flat Slavic face, but I do
have his eyes; the skin
folds over the corners
in the same way.

When he's tired
he rubs his top lip
with his middle finger
in an obscene gesture.

When I feel the same itch
I think of smoothness
and find something to do
with my hands.

Window

My son makes no fuss in his sudden change of circumstance,
merely explores the new sensation with his long fingers,
searches out his mother's breast with a curious mouth.

Outside the evening is taking hold, I see myself
in the window, in the sky with the moon
and all the paraphernalia of the maternity room.

My father fills a glass with whisky, washes down
all his pills, lies on the counterpane
and watches the lampshade fade.

He awakes to the smell of latex, his right eye
stretched open by a doctor's forefinger and thumb,
the ward slowly becoming familiar.

Whistle

The undertaker
plumps his cheeks,
which purses his lips.

It's as if my father
is about to whistle.

Sausages

Every time we visit my wife's mother
in Luton, I find myself scooting
round the corner to the Polish shop.
It has shelves of sauerkraut in jars
and strings of sausages in a cabinet.

Sometimes they don't get home,
I dip them into the jar of mustard
as I drive, and eat them cold.

The Shed

stands immutable,
eyes milky with cobwebs
looks back with no flicker
of recognition.

Behind its latch,
paint tins
and forgotten things
not fit for the house.

Hot Day

I stoop through brambles
into a scratched photograph.

Along the path, shirtless boys
wet from the river.

The pool I swam in forty years ago is dry,
the ground broken apart.

I reach down
and put my hand into it.

Dad's Alma Mater

squats on a low hill at the end of a Berkshire lane,
watches the moor with its many eyes, keeps thoughts
inside heads, inside rooms, behind walls, behind wire.

A deer breaks from the gorse
shakes rain from yellow flowers,
I remember being small.

Distance

Suddenly June catches her breath,
wakes reeling from the vertiginous
blurred curvature of the earth,
its unappeasable distance
where she hangs, voiceless.

Below, lines of silver
slowly pull into focus,
she sees three rivers.

These rivers are survivors
coursing through canyons
of beasts and wild flowers
like blood through veins.

They carry her with them.
This isn't a dream.